101* Lumpy Love Poems.

LOVE & CHIPS.

Fractured Fervidness and Unction Unleashed.
A Tottering Triumph of Turgididity.

BY

The famous unknown,

ROGER HOWARTH

With Additional Creative Input from

JONATHAN ROYLE

LOVE & CHIPS.

Dedicated to all those languishing amongst the lost luggage of love.

LOVE & CHIPS.
Copyright Jonathan Royle 2019
Copyright: Roger Howarth. 2003

1

I love your beautiful complexion,
Like permanent blue ink,
Eyes that change direction,
And uncontrollably blink.
That bottom, like house bricks in a sack,
God, I'm turned on by your woollen vest,
Nightly, I see you on your back,
A challenge, like Everest. Will I ever?

2

It's our anniversary once again,
So a few words from the heart,
Is it possible to have one precious days refrain,
From a burp, a sniffle, or a fart.
But how can I claim such cause to regret,
A mystery of Life now clear,
For now I know the great secret,
Of why God invented beer.

3

Darling, may I please insist,
You stop cutting your toe-nails in bed,
And did a time really ever exist,
When you had teeth somewhere in your head. Good night my love.

4

My treasured trampoline,
Where have you been,
Such a gymnasium of form,
Way above the norm.
My precious pole vault,
Who could fault,
Such climbing nets of grace,
As traverse your face.
My holy high beam,
A marathon dream,
A pentathlon, Heaven sent,
Oh please, be my equestrian event.

5

Be my Wellington boots, dearest,
Protecting me from Life's puddles,
Be my night club bouncer, sweetest,
To sort out my mix ups and muddles, snuddles.

6

You are the mountain I need to climb,
My cheap day return to worlds sublime,
And you are the drizzle that sweetens summer days,
The frizzle of bacon, that says,
"I'm done".
Love, I'm ready to be burned,
By your sun.

7

You are the steam in my kettle,
The Brasso for my mettle,
You're the Baby Bio for the flowers,
In the garden of my soul.
You are the hole,
I need to fill in my life,
The butter,
For my spiritual knife.

8

When God designed you, my love,
He was smashed out of his head,
Angels must have wiped their bums on the plans,
Enough said.

9

Oh darling, be my Nivia cream,
I'm burning under love's gleam,
Spread your dream,
Over me and my yearning.
Dos't you hear my scream,
Woulds't you have me lie here and steam,
Under every sunbeam you stream,
Oh please, use your expertise,
To end this endless sauntering.

10

If God made underpants,
He'd make them just like you,
The comfort and support,
That lasts a whole life through.
For a man needs holding up,
In so many hidden ways,
So be my Y Fronts baby,
And end these low down days.

11

I'm trapped on Life's downward escalator,
Crawling up, but it's moving too fast,
You're at the top, calling,
I know I just can't last.
Please press the stop button,
Jump into my humble shopping bag,
I don't want the bargain basement,
I want you,
But not the price tag.

12

Love is like breaking wind,
It can take you by surprise,
Embarrass you in public,
Make you turn from questioning eyes.
But you're the biggest burp of my life,
My angel of flatulence,
For you, I'll barf forever,
And leave the rest to chance.
So join me in Life's endeavour,
To relieve the pressures of each day,
Let us break wind together,
And blow Life's cares away.

13

My little buttered muffin,
That waits for me tonight,
So soft and round and eatable,
And I will have first bite.
For this is love with jam on it,
I hunger just for you,
Your dough has risen beautifully,
And you're oven bottomed too.

14

Love is like a breeze,
Upon a wave,
Picked up by persons,
To whom that love you gave.
But if your love should have one small flaw,
To widen, to a cave,
It will not survive,
The journey on the wave,
The bloody thing will sink.

15

You are the crouton that adds richness,
To the cuppasoup of my life,
A crouton perfection,
Titivating toasted confection,
    To be dunked in and out,
Without doubt,
You are a crouton to moot on.

16

My heart is like a bathtub, filled,
With steaming waters, stilled,
In readiness for your ablution,
The only solution,
To whip up those soapy gallons of love.
Step in. Have a scrub,
And that little flying cherub, Cupid,
Will sponge all doubt away,
In the tub of love you'll stay,
For ever. Never,
To pull the plug.

17

Like the starship Enterprise,
You warped into my realm,
As we looked into each others eyes,
Captain love was at the helm.
You've caught me in your tractor beam,
Pulling on impulse power,
We're not the aliens we seem,
As photons of passion shower.
Beam me to your buffers now,
My tricorder says I must,
Your coils will reach warp factor, 'WOW',
As I phaser you with lust.

18

My love is like Elastoplast,
It hides the cuts of living,
It helps to heal the wounds and scars,
That fate seems keen on giving.
And so, my little aspirin, be also my Germolene,

Forever your T.C.P. I'll be,
More than a lover, a poultice to cover,
My sore heart,
Be a first aid kit to me.

19

Your hair, dewy turf. Eyes, footballs,
Scoring goals in my heart each day,
Your body is the stadium of my life,
I beg you, don't play away.
Those legs, as goal posts,
Waiting for the winning try,
Watch the centre forward my love,
Don't let one slip by.
Save the back of the net for me,
My extra time is worth the wait,
For I will score form your off side,
And win on aggregate.

20

Love you more than pickled eggs,
Love you more than clothes pegs,
Love you more than wooded legs,
Love you more than warts and segs.
That's some love baby.

21

Just to say:
Waves lapped my feet as I gazed o'er the sea,
I trod on a jellyfish, and thought of thee,

For like that flattened Man of War I would become,
If you should leave me.
And as the sunset gilded space,
I blew up my lilo, and saw your face,
For the airbed of my heart would fill with grief,
Ever you would leave me.
Now, in the twilight, lying there,
A pile of seaweed, shining. Lo! Your gelled hair,
For the kelp of my soul would sway far away,
How could you leave me.
Accept these words, sealed with a kiss,
Stay for ever. Of course you will,
Mine still,
Who else could write as good as this?

22

Oh cherry fluff, my woolly Balaclava,
When puff the chill winds of Fate to tickle my ears,
You give enough, sweet pickle, my dredger. Be good,
Clear the mud,
From so many lonely years.

23

Oh snuggle fruit, the gas meter for my heart's lonely room,
Bringing sweeter warmth to parts where there was none,
Darling passion bubble. My Kenwood blender,
So tender with the mixing,
Fixing with gentle thumps,
Till all the bumps and lumps of Life are gone.
My cuddle pudding,
I want for nudding.

24

If you were a packet of crisps, my love,
Plain flavoured some might say,
I'd be your little blue salt bag,
And sprinkle you night and day.
They can keep all their fancy flavours,
Crinkle cuts, chips sticks have I tried,
You're the no nonsense crunch that I long for,
A packet full, and well fried.

25

I love you as no other can,
I love you like my frying pan,
For without it I could not fry bacon,
Oh why must my love be so forsaken.
Easy.

26

Your eyes shine like traffic lights,
Permanently on go,
Should I have to put breaks on,
With no warning saying slow.
Your body is like a motorway,
For sporty cars reserved,
Please be my service station,
Where love and chips are served.

27

Sweet refreshing crystals of purity, (snow)
Greet the Earth after gentle fall, (It's snowing)
And become intimate, (Have sex)
With the naked womanliness of trees, (Barking)

That softly sway their outstretched nets, (Branches)
To try to catch them all,
As I try to catch you. (No chance. Not with a tree)

28

The sun which lights our days is shamed,
By your radiance each morning,
And when you put your teeth in, after yawning,
Oh transports of turgid titillation,
What a sensation,
The miracle is complete,
With smelly feet.
A divine creature in string pants and vest,
Is now manifest. Coughing up over the sink. A symphony,
To the brewery,
No jury could condemn the breaking of your wind,
It is a fanfare to the heavens, and to the curry shop,
Should I stop now? No. Your belching is in harmony with the celestial
spheres,
Too many beers, mirrored in your bloodshot eyes,
No surprise if angels should swoop to comfort you,
As you poop and throw up yet again in the sink,
What a hell bourn stink, but those angels don't care,
They smooth your matted hair,
Whilst mere mortals go about their day,
That saintly head you lay, once more in the curry tray.
To scratch and cough. Spit and shit,
Stink a bit, think of it,
A true Olympian of idleness in our midst,
Pissed. Eyes shine. Too divine for mere Earthly labours.

29

You are the booster rocket,
On the space ship of Life,
To which I hold a tether,
You are the push I need,
That woosh of warp speed,
To send me through,
Like a vindaloo, the black hole of each day,
I yearn,
Don't burn out on me. Stay, I prey,
In orbit,
The beauty, absorb it,
Let's try for re-entry together.

30

My beautiful balloon,
Blown up with love,
May I swoon,
Fly high above,
With you.
Be true,
I am no ballast to be dropped in flight,
Be my Goodyear blimp, tonight.

31

There's something I ought to tell you,
When I pass water, yes, I can smell you,
Especially when passing a twinkling stream,
Or a misty lake, as if in a passing dream,
Not forgetting the secret woodland pond,
Your scent goes far beyond,
The mortal senses. Yet the strongest fragrances of thee,
Comes when I'm passing by the sea.
So pass off.

32

Darling pudding chips and peas,
Served with gravy, in a tray,
Your beauty, more wondrous than these,
Scant offerings, from Life's take-away.
You, a crinkle cut? Not right,
To leave your charms unsung,
Be my poppadom tonight,
And I'll be your king prawn foo yung.
We could be the foo yung ones.

33

The chip shop of my mind,
Filled with cod and plaice,
Yet through it all I seem to find,
Your golden deep fried face.
Please wrap me up, I beg you,
On these battered bended knees,
Be the dumpling in my humble stew,
My pudding chips and peas.

34

Darling nose drip,
How can I show my love,
Shall I faint,
Or poetically paint,
Sweet words,
To give our love a shove.
Oh how your toes grip,
My heart, so shredded,
Can't express it,
Should I suppress it,
And dream of us being wedded,
No, sod it,
Dream of us being bedded.

35

There is a lump I need to get rid of,
It's growing day by day,
Like a saint, you arrived,
And I have survived,
With this lump that won't go away.
Oh angel, let me share this lump with you,
And with all my treasures I will part,
There's no way of telling,
The size of the swelling,
This lump of love fills my heart.

36

Love you to the power of ten,
Love you now and love you then,
Love you since I don't know when,
Love you all over again. Phew!

37

I sit and watch the clouds go by,
Scudding swiftly across the sky,
And lo, a little bird sings twit twit,
Then zooms past and drops a bit,
Of worm,
From it's little beak,
And some inner voice does speak,
For that little bird is thee,
And the worm is me,
Dropped from your life.

38

A word of worming.
No bird could love a worm more,
I'm worm sodden with love for you,
Nor could I drop you to the floor,
This I could not, wormld not do.
For you are the worm in the beak of my love,
Now, by wormlight, back to my place of rest,
Let us fly and seek so high above,
My nest. As food? Nay, as a guest.
For only with worm love my heart is fed,
This bird, with worming lies ne'er deceives,
Impressed? Who wormn't be,
Or could say that style was dead,
Could Keats so repeats so, amongst the twigs and leaves?

39

I see you and I turn to jelly,
Don't treat me like a worn out wellie,
For my love soars as a fireworks display,
You can light my Roman candle any day. I'll even provide the matches.

40

Love is like taking a photograph,
It can make you cry, or make you laugh,
Sometimes the lighting is too bright,
Or your focus, just not quite right.
It can also make you scream and shout,
The great moment arrives, but the film runs out,
Ah, but then, when the development is done,
So oft is wished the lens cap had remained firm on.

41

Oh Susan,
If I could choose one,
She would be just like you,
Oh Susan,
Such a face to peruse on,
What am I to do?
Oh Susan,
Where has all the booze gone,
I need some escape,
Oh Susan,
Why must Life cruise on,
Why can't I video tape,
Your loveliness,
And then I'll never loose one,
As wonderful,
As Susan.

42

As a sweet bird of love I hover to and fro,
Watching your shining head below,
And such a turn on. No sign of hair,
It makes the target easier.

43

Last night I dreamt you were a rag pudding. I was kissing each safety
pin,
And thinking of all the chunky goodness wrapped carefully within,
You were boiled up with passion and served. To your rags I did
daintily attend,
A feast of pleasure awaiting? No, just a great big gormless end. *

* Northern slang. The parts of a suet pudding with no meat. Useless. A stupid situation or person. Idiotic.

44

If I had a penny,
For each time I thought of you and romance,
I'd be a multimillionaire by now,
And you wouldn't stand a chance.
My mansion to live in. Fast cars. A jet.
A yacht beneath stars that glint.
Instead, why not take me as I am,
In love with you, and skint.

45

Jason,
The race is on,
I'll set the pace on Jason.
Jason,
I wouldn't disgrace one,
I'll put my best face on, for Jason.
Jason,
I'm a 'know my place' one,
But no straight lace one,
So come on,
Jason.

46

Please accept this written token,
For all the words left unspoken,
Words that I now could choke on,
Some would have left my heart unbroken.
I'm the one Fate chooses to have a joke on,
Now sadness keeps it's heavy yoke on,
And helps me pull this unhappy cloak on,
As a rain storm of tears threaten to soak one.
This bloke on his own.

47

Yesterday I burned the chip pan,
And I remember how our love began,
A smouldering passion, then a woosh,
The first time my hands fell on your tush.
The smoke rose up, flames roared,
As did our melted spirits soared,
And like that chip pan, raging, our minds a fuzz,
Until Fate threw a wet towel over us.

48

Oh Amanda,
Let me not bander,
Words. I'm soft on you,
Like a balloon, I swoon,
Aloft on you.
Oh Amanda,
You command a,
Special place at the breakfast table of my heart,
Always able,
Right from the start.
Oh Amanda,
If I could meander,

Through this life again,
Kiss the heartache and pain,
And demand a,
Amanda.

49

Oh Lydia, I'm feeling giddier,
At the thought of you belonging to me,
Oh Lydia, so highly I consider yer,
Please say you'll come home for tea,
We could have a toasted muffin,
Or a covert buttered scone,
And then, a little trifle,
To make you my own,
Oh Lydia, I'd never get rid of yer,
Lead me to that alter door,
Oh Lydia, please, no perfidia,
You're the one my heart beats for.

50

The petals of a rose,
Which grows by a stream,
And have fallen in the waters there,
Each as a silent prayer to the moon,
At that same time, a shield,
To yield the sun's light upon it's face,
Many million years now worn.
And the moon's reflected light,
Dissects the night with magic splinters,
Echoes of phantom winters where laughter dies,
And my heart cries, broken,
Words left unspoken. To fall within the moonlight dance,
No backward glance. The petals take them all,
Many million tears now born.

51

I was on the loo the other day,
Nothing new to do that you might say,
But within the sacred confines of that bog,
Memories, like this constipation, began to jog,
The anticipation of our first date,
As I sit here, I could not wait,
To hear your laughter roar,
Just like my arse, we laughed ourselves soar,
Just as today there blew a wind,
Love unchained, unrestrained, drained, not to rescind,
Flushed with youth,
Blushed with truth,
Unravelled, like this Andrex,
My love, so complex,
My soul, never moved like this before,
As I carve your name into this door,
For others to see,
To make them feel completely free,
Loose,
To let fly their deepest thought,
The face contorts,
In pain, again.
Love, down the drain.

52

Why?
Do I wait,
Beneath the shadows of words,
Which drift by me,
As I sit here, with nothing,
Beside me, save loveless space.
In state,
As the mists of dreams,
And flowers of lost hope,
Appear before my tortured eyes,

No more to see your face.
To hate,
The heart that beats alone,
In helpless wonderment,
At loosing once again,
And falling far from grace.
To create,
A youless world around me,
Where once I sent you poems,
Such as this. Now I kiss the breeze,
And no more run the race. Why?

53

The heart,
That was once within me,
Now lies and dies in ashes before me,
As I gaze down, with reddened eyes,
Gunged up, as though jammed with pearls, of crystal glass,
The lips,
That wantonly, shamelessly, recklessly, adorn my face,
Have no further use, now that they cannot unite,
With your perfected orifice,
But can only utter pathetic sounds of love,
And hands,
No more to touch such buxomness,
Can only wave goodbye to dreams,
Or hold the hankie for my runny nose,
And write pathetic words of love.

54

Be mine,
The pebble on the beach,
Is as a person, alone. Get it?
For though it is surrounded,
By others on that beach,

The pebble dare not move,
Dare not cry out,
Or write a super poem such as this.
It is too afraid, should it be seen,
And placed in a museum,
For all to stare and laugh.
So the pebble (ME) stays alone,
It's talents unsung. It's love for you in chains,
Until the tide unites them all,
And they are washed down together,
Into the sea of time.
Be mine.
It doesn't come much better than this baby.

55

My life. Each bit,
As a day when the fairy sugared surface,
Of a quartz mirror lake,
Shone. Reflecting the hazed white blueness,
Of an untouched silk sky,
And the wind of my days was asleep,
Nothing to disturb,
The tranquil peacefulness of it all,
Until the bomb of my love for you hit.
Shit.

56

I am as a flower with one tiny petal,
Guarding it so tenderly,
To see,
That this precious frail possession,
Must come to no harm.
I care so deeply for its protection,
Its health and happiness,
Yes,

You are this tiny beautiful petal.
And should you ever leave my stem,
Leave my pistils bare,
I swear. As a tear falls, so shall I,
And the flower of me will die. So there.

57

The moon is phosphorus white,
Which monotones the Earth,
I'm at it again, for all I'm worth,
Writing. Fringed with luminous yellow,
Turning blue and green,
The Earth is seen.
The sky, a perfect untextured surface,
As my writing pad,
For a beginner, not bad. A hazed matt grey,
Viewed through tear filled eyes.
Pierced with the points of white hot needles, the skies,
Spelling out figures, shapes,
A hunter, lion, a great bear, trainers, your name,
All for me to gaze upon,
Now you're gone, and the air is quiet and asleep,
And the monotone Earth rests with it,
But I cannot,
What have I got? My poems,
Now that you have left me.

58

The pool has lost its beauty,
And no more reflects the skies,
The sun is dulled upon it,
Now cold and shivering lies.
The willow, known for weeping,
Now even harder cries,
I stand beneath those tears of green,
As the wind, in mourning, sighs.

The swallow has stopped singing,
No more through cloud flies,
I know I have lost you my love,
At my feet, love's flower dies.

59

My darling U.F.O.,
A 'thing' from way up there,
Please land on my emotions,
You close encounterer.
Don't U.F.O. without me,
Into the vast unknown,
My space drive will take a dive,
For I cannot warp alone.

60

In frozen animation, a millennium of forms,
Lie crisp and deep and white, tinted with feminine pink,
From a lemon orange orb, which floats with precision,
As does the balance of a clock,
My pendulum swings for you.

61

Let me give to you a petal,
And then you can take my leaf,
For we run through Life together,
In time, alas, too brief.
So my love for you I'll show,
In my naff poetic way,
You're going to get a great big petal,
Each and every day.

62

A day with sweet subtlety now dawns,
I awaken too,
Refreshed with dreamfull slumber,
To greet the day anew.
I walk through the hours of dawning,
Across fields of crystalline dew,
And there, in mists of silver dust,
My thoughts now turn to you.
The one who did a runner,
Our love, thwarted. It never grew,
As daylight breaks I ponder,
On dreams I never knew.
I'm leaving now, as the night pulls back,
Like the last star, so far you flew,
Back to the van where I can get dressed,
For the sky and I are turning blue.

63

I stand in the bepuddled wilderness of Life,
Watching. My systems way off line,
As the mists of Time, like steam from a freshly formed cow pat,
In irradiant, technoshock, particles,
Collide with mine.
I land on a desert of unruffled eloquence,
Filled with the ghosts of lonely trees,
Who sway their branches in a none existent wind,
As I turn away my Time worn eyes,
From these, so many once were mees.
Help at hand! A surfeit of angels, in Specsavers specials,
Crash beam around my flatulent head,
Offering me bitter Bendicks peppermints of wisdom,
Some thick blob shop wine of knowledge,
Too late. Sadness now is my only bread.

64

Leaves,
Blowing like the remnants of Christmas trimmings,
Against my window pane,
As I sit here in pain. Sifting my thoughts through the blender of hopes,
That may not rise again.
Leaves,
Each one a loving, backbreaking, carpet ripping kiss,
Each twig and stem, a beer,
Blowing through the midden of each day,
Without you near.
Leaves,
Each one a lost moment of shoe throwing happiness,
Carpeting the cobbles of my existence with a lonely sludge,
Like giant soggy crisps. As the sun turns into a busted child's balloon,
To my empty home I trudge.

65

Autumn leaves, drifting slowly,
Like lost feathers from a bird's wing,
To the ground,
A breeze, growing colder,
As the season matures,
Now comes to disturb,
And blow them all around.
I watch them go,
Dancing like puppets,
From gossamer strings,
Through the frightening night.
I think of you,
Walking out of sight,
With that turd I thought was a mate.

66

Little droplets of moisture,
Which bring this news,
Cemented between walls of liquid film,
On which my sad story is told,
Are carnaged on pavements,
After one fatal cascade,
Or still hang in populace profusion,
Like tiny honey lozenges of dire truth,
Which are fated to fall upon my lies,
And try to inoculate the land,
From fragrances of my evil deed.
Sorry.

67

I dream of you as a great pan of dumplings and stew,
Lust and desires bubbling away,
Then from the hotplate of passion I'll take my fair ration,
Oh yes, you can sit in my microwave any day.

68

Who could make a rose more beautiful,
Or fly, unaided, through the sky,
Who could hold the moon between their hands,
Or make tides wait,
And who has seen a flower cry.
Who could blow a tree down with a kiss,
Catch a snowflake on a pin,
Or begin to love you more than I.

69

A stagnant whirlpool of distant echoes,
Laughter, coughing and people throwing up,
Surrounds and dolbyfies my blitzed head,
Crushing the last dog ends of your image,
From my technocrazed mind.
A jovial cloud drops it's load on me,
Drenched,
And all feelings, lustings, hungerings and mooings,
That were caged just for you,
Are car washed away.
On suds of stupidity,
The dismal dinner of my dreams floats off,
A mad meaningless meal,
As the laughing sun sheds it's heavy light,
My love, like chips in a golden gutter.

70

From a well in my heart,
A watery flame of love,
As pink as the embers of a day,
Falls up along golden tubes,
Lined with the petals of orchids,
Perfumed with fragrances,
Of gentle tenderness,
To reach my lips,
So that my love can flow to you,
In one great big sloppy kiss.

71

You're missed,
And the sun is setting like concrete in my eyes,
Which are giving birth to the liquid fruits of fedupness,
My heart is drained, rinsed out, flushed and detoxed,

Of all the tender pastel twinkly blotches of happiness.
My mind is a knackered kaleidoscope of treasured events,
Which now drift too far away,
To be heard, felt, seen, tripped over or sat on.
I'm pissed.

72

Oh my love. Oh my love, my love, my turbo boosted love,
My love is wasted.
Oh your lips. Oh your lips, your lips,
Your sweet green lips,
I should have tasted.
Oh your bum. Oh your bum, your bum,
Your firm round 'got to grab it' bum,
I could have pasted.
Oh my end. Oh my end, my end,
My fruitless, needless, end,
By this waste is hasted.

73

Sadness pains, my love,
Pain which truly puts the mystic boot in,
Again, twixt heart and soul and living sequin tear,
When near to the untouchable you,
So much about you, unknown,
To own just one shining particle,
Of such an article as your hair,
I dare not imagine it for fear of bringing,
The awesome clinfilming pain.
Of loving you in vain.

74

There you stand, so lovely,
So grand and lovely and big,
In girth, as the planet Earth, seen with a sheen,
Of blue, you from afar are.
You are mine as the stars are mine,
Let our lights entwine. Our spirits dine,
On all their size and splendour,
In sweet rapport. Who could want more,
Yet the planets are mirrored in your sumptuous form,
Each crater made greater, each tectonic rift a gift,
How my heart sings, seeing all those rings,
And things from outer space,
Your face, no time warp could displace,
Oh what nights,
All mine. A galaxy of delights.

75

There you are, my antililiquil love,
And I kiss you debundantly,
As I would kiss the polyvestle spaceiarch,
The catacolonic celestial force,
Which credits us with Life.
Space and time, and a few chip papers,
Revolve around us,
A vast dewdropian continuum of things trying not to be,
As mysterious as the last statement,
Profound in their lack of all,
Carrying us up,
Beyond the reaches of porticious aximortal contention,
As we love,
And get smashed together.

76

Beautiful bubble of love, don't break,
Take me through your Elysian air,
But please make sure that I fly through magic sky,
In clean socks and underwear.

77

Your image reaches through my heart,
You make me want to drop a part,
They call a tear,
Oh such profanity,
When I see you, my mind goes blank,
Rush to the bathroom and start to thank,
The thing I hold most dear…my sanity.

78

Oh why these memories of you I keep,
Always the dreamer,
And you, a steamer, sitting low in the water,
Sailing rampant o'er love's anguished seas,
Trailing the rags,
Of my time scalded emotions,
Clobbering and Kung Fooing,
My oven ready wooing,
Undoing all the laces in my heart,
Until a cry is heard,
Like some prehistoric bird,
And I am seen to weep. Happy now?

79

To your hair, my regard,
The swaled grass of Life's young springtime,
Caught on the breaking of Nature's timeless wind,
For but a reckless instant of divine time,
Then to crash back,
Like a sack of magic chains,
To it's resting place,
The sacred pencil lined canyon,
Of thy facade.

80

This April day,
Let me kiss your galactic lower lip,
Is that timeless Love I sip,
Or last nights cosmic curry,
No space warping hurry,
As I taste upon them,
The waste upon them,
And you laugh, so alien and insanely,
So meteorlistic and astrogainly,
As we lock on extremities and embrace,
Let me kiss your planetary face,
This April day,
Mirror of the moon,
A festoon of craters,
There to elate as,
I hold you in my arms,
And your star sodden hair, set loose,
From the mousse of time and space,
Displace with tangled efficiency,
The trivial doings of each mortal event,
You are the Universe, in a tent,
This April day.

81

See,
Your eyes,
Like two stir fries,
Unpumable pools of delight,
One might assume with delicious liquids filled,
Rightly thrilled,
Hot love jelly,
Clear and wobbling,
Hear my slobbering,
Springtime's Life beating rap,
Full to overflowing,
Mine for the knowing,
This jelly of love in the wok of your eyes,
I don't care what the stock or flavour,
Gladly to savour,
Rich gustatorial delights bestow,
And I'll just let them flow,
Over me.

82

Let me think on your lips,
Drink on your lips,
Full of Life's trumpeting song,
And they belong to me,
Bon appetit. A rubeus brooch,
That mocks the sun's fiery setting,
Electric shocks with Love's begetting,
But more than this,
The angels above on cloud,
However loud, could not voice a more perfect sound,
As that which from your lips does fartingly expound,
How does it go,
That song I, oh so well, know,
So oft I've heard those sacred words,
Verbal love birds, edict,

Within the temple of my mind, on walls writ,
Lips strict edict I merit,
"You've got five minutes. Get on with it."

83

Oh little bubble of dreams,
Centre of all my schemes,
It seems that fate teams us far apart.
And when the sunlight gleams,
With radiant sparkling beams,
Tears flow out in streams,
Poetry in reams,
And hope redeems my broken heart.

84

And I have kissed you,
In my dreams I have kissed those cherub twins,
Of all the sins,
I long for this,
A kiss, with all the fruitiness,
That one poor beer sodden heart can give,
So let me live,
For the moment,
That bright chunk of nutty slack,
Set in Time's eternal belt,
When we shall kiss for real.

85

With brilliant chip pan on fire fury burns the shuttle's primeval thrust,
Reaching its gut dropping escape velocity burst,
Plumes of mind claim flame Heaven bound,

Severing Earthly forces with ear riveting sound,
So, likewise, my love burns the duvet of time and space for thee.
G forces, tranquil, beer spill awe instil at the grace and precision,
Of the space station, orbiting, sans derision,
But the grace your solar panelled body does command,
Challenges all human mind to understand,
As the anti gravity problem, it solves.
Revolves the Earth unaware as strange saucer craft approach,
From deep space, our customs and web sites to poach,
All high techno-how ensnared,
Yet still, seeing you, those aliens are so unprepared,
Leaving skid marks on space in retreat. Defeat.

86

I'm so hard with love.
Why am I barred from love,
Is it something I've done or said.
Is it the clothes that I wear,
The style of my hair,
Or the honesty of wanting you in bed.
I'm so scarred with love,
Feathered and tarred with love,
Yet you tease as you please, hurting so.
I don't wear a padlock through my ear,
Yet you avoid and stay clear,
With the two fingered euphemism for go.
I'm so marred with love,
Lost, storm tossed and ill starred with love,
Over my passion, the dirty water of contempt pours,
Would a single lottery win,
Send your heart in a spin,
Well I have. A roll-over. Now it's your turn to. My place or yours.

87

Oh is this Love that I do feel,
Is Love to blame and gives its name to the gormless rider,
Who fires Love's dart on a phantom cart horse,
Galloping within the tumble drier, deep fat fryer, of my stomach.
Oh is this Love from which I reel,
Is Love the force which does awaken and has taken it's Terminator
boots off,
Resting it's steaming sweaty feet on the neat buffet of my emotions,
Stinking out the curtained rooms of that part which is the heart.
Oh is this Love, my senses to steal,
Is Love the name of the demented fermented split jeans rock band,
Exploding instruments and defecating sound abound,
Within the vaulted exalted swimming pool of my mind.
If Love be it…shit.

88

What is that bird,
Which nightly sings from the longing tree,
Then to fly forth on a prayer,
Through mind and soul,
Perchance to find my lips,
And lay it's eggs of desire upon them.
Or does imagination disturb that saintly bird,
Nay, this is for real,
That is the bird of Love which sings,
And I had better catch it quick,
Lest foul fate awake its evil eye,
And next doors cat gets it.

89

How to describe you, in one word,
That's not absurd or slurred,
Must fit the bill. Inspiration spurred,
Perhaps even thrill, loins to gird.

A word conferred with emotion stirred,
Concurred with tearful vision blurred,
A brilliant lingual star, feelings inferred,
I go too far. Poetry murd-ered.
Yet now, a word has just occurred,
And to your grace it is transferred,
Keep secret? No. I'm not deterred,
These feelings must show. A secret shared.
Thus, softly whispered now, and not with guilt impaired,
But with impassioned breath, sweet golden nothing, murmured,
Let the describing word at last be heard.
You, my darling, are a turd.

90

Oh Pearl, you're the girl,
Who makes my hair curl, my heart swirl,
My wildest dreams unfurl, my days pass in a whirl,
My eyes twirl. Never to be churl if you say that there'll, always be
Pearl.

91

And now, to knickers most chaste, I compare thy face,
Your smile, lo, tis that trim of lace,
Embroidered strands of fine elastic,
Your hair, equally fantastic.
Nose, ears, those delicate stitched motifs,
Tis no mere plain pair of briefs,
Comparing thee, I now fully suss it,
Your chin, beloved, a double gusset.
Eyes, how could they ever vex,
When seen through sensual airtex,
Skin, fresh and white, as the virgin cotton,
Love hangs before us, with not a lot on.

92

If you were a mobile phone my love,
My bill would be a fright,
I'd be pressing your call button,
Morning noon and night.
A leather case of course, and vibra mode,
As you hang fetchingly from my belt,
Waiting for your silent, secret call,
And secret tremors felt.
If you were a mobile phone my love,
I'd press each digit with care,
Across seas and mountains, town and country,
I'd make calls on you any and everywhere.
A Motorola Startack, classic,
To me that's how you'll always seem,
A quick flip and you're ready to use,
As I dream of your digital stream.

93

Without being rude, or crude, but if you were food,
You'd be almost too good for mortal lips,
But what celestial consommé done with magical aplomb,
Would my taste buds of passion get to grips.
Angel's cake with sun rays perhaps. Some divine take-aways perhaps,
Through this menu of dream dishes one skips,
Until I turn the page and my hunger of need does enrage,
There you are, my rag pudding of love, with chips.

94

And so, you are my washing line,
On which the clothes of my soul hang to dry,
The shrunken woolly jumper of my dreams,
My best shirt of hope, frayed at the seams,
Blow beneath a hapless sky.

I'm pegged out for you, rain or shine,
Clinging on, least anything falls,
Darned socks of desire. Tattered jeans of trust,
Torn T-shirts of tears, perilous above the dust,
Hang with my love void vest, and all the rest of my emotional smalls.

95

I'd like to know, before I go, with words that rhyme and flow,
If you'll visit my garden shed,
Which is a round about way and just being silly to say,
I've got you inside my head.
No, shed is not the word, but I'm scared of this secret shared,
And dread I might loose my street cred,
But no caution can dissuade it, no reason has delayed it,
So write it down and let it be read.
Oh which word do I seek that is making me weak,
Rhymes with shed, at times with head, dread, cred, read and dead,
Let's throw in bread for good measure and my uncle Fred, whom I
treasure,
But it's not him I want in my - .
See, very nearly, beginning, sinning, with that letter - . It will get the
better of me,
How dangerously this poetic road I tread,
But would it be such a catastrophe,
If that three letter word were said.
Oh sod it, I'll do it. If I'm spurned I'll get through it,
Though all of my dreams will have fled,
I'd like to know, before I go, with words that rhyme and flow,
If you'll visit, not my shed, but instead be lead to my bed.

96

I'm no Shakespeare my dear,
But I'll do my best through the tempest to make words fit,
Measure for measure you're my greatest treasure,
Which I keep praying is just as you like it.
2 B or not 2 B,

Yes, the classroom where first we met. How quaint,
So long ago and my mood is as black as Othello,
For I still have a lover's complaint.
I'm star crossed and tossed with love's labours lost,
This is my twelfth night in the rain,
Watching your window with terrors as the comedy of errors,
Means much ado about nothing, again.

97

I've made a great big puddle,
Along Life's stony lane,
I'm going to jump straight into it,
Again.
This puddle of love lies waiting,
Just for me and you,
I'll be the first to sit down in it,
Please say you'll get wet too.
My wellies are flooded with passion,
I'm soaked in the mud of desire,
Won't you please sit down beside me,
Let's hold hands in the mire.
But now I stand beside my puddle,
Waiting for you to give me a shove,
Hoping you'll fall in with me,
So we can cuddle in the puddle of love.

98

No-one could love you more than me,
I'd sacrifice my Sunday tea,
A crystal clear glass of beer,
Wouldn't shed a tear,
Just to be near,
Thee.

No-one could need you more than I,
More than a golden crusted pie,
Filled with steak. Don't love forsake,
My heart will ache,
Then break,
And die.
This love, Heaven alone should beget it,
Take all I own. I wouldn't regret it,
My kecks and socks, A panoplies,
In context, my stocks of Nana C.D.s,
On bended knees, please, take all these.
No. I only tease. Forget it.

99

You little satellite dish,
How I wish that you'd broadcast to me,
Every channel of delight,
Tuned to annul the plight,
Of wanting to be your T.V.
I'm waiting with my wide screen,
So you'd be seen at your surroundsound best,
Then let us cut all the flannel,
And get us to your sports channel,
The button that would get the most pressed.

100

The sun is yet an infant in the sky,
Fields, still filled with treasured mist,
And swallows stir their wings to fly,
As the tops of trees with golden magic kissed,
Colour, now a blessing being given,
The sky, a curtain being withdrawn,
Yet shadows still mock the feathers of a raven,
Where I wait for you at dawn.

101

Oh Brenda,
Let me be your defender,
My love I will tender,
Let me be the only contender,
With a heart to render,
Emotions to surrender,
Your broken dreams,
Let me be the mender,
Your sweet nothings sender,
Oh Brenda,
I'm on a bender, for you.

102*

In the great cosmic commode that we know as life,
I drift with all manner of cares and strife,
Within the astral cesspit of mortal dreams,
Where all my plans and schemes,
For love,
Are wiped away by the great toilet roll of time,
With all reason and rhyme,
Flushed by fate's great cistern tanks,
But still I sit here, giving thanks,
To see beyond life's loo door and still glimpse your face,
That fortune's u bend tries to send without a trace,
Into the mystic sewerage works of aspiration,
Still, my expectation,
To be dumped on yet again, by love.

THE END.

At Last. Aghast,
Steadfast emotions outcast,
Can this go on,
Has all reason gone,
Sanities sail, blown from reason's mast,
But what a blast.

103*

DiCaprio, that Romeo,
Your angel incognito,
Oh tell me it isn't so,
That I could never glow like Leonardo.
Where do I have to go,
What tricks do I need to know,
Which hand do I have to show,
Or the winning dice I need to throw.
Which line do I have to tow,
How many meadows of dreams shall I mow,
Seeds of hope sow,
An orchestra of poetic trumpets such as this must I blow.
If so, prey then you might listen and break the status quo,
Thus left unheard, I'm thrown by anguish, to and fro,
Fated to stoop, but knowing not how low,
Oh what will make your affections grow.
Your favours, I prey, you might bestow,
And thus it is me, no, not Leo,
Who becomes your fantasy intacto,
Your very real dream bow.

The Very End.
****